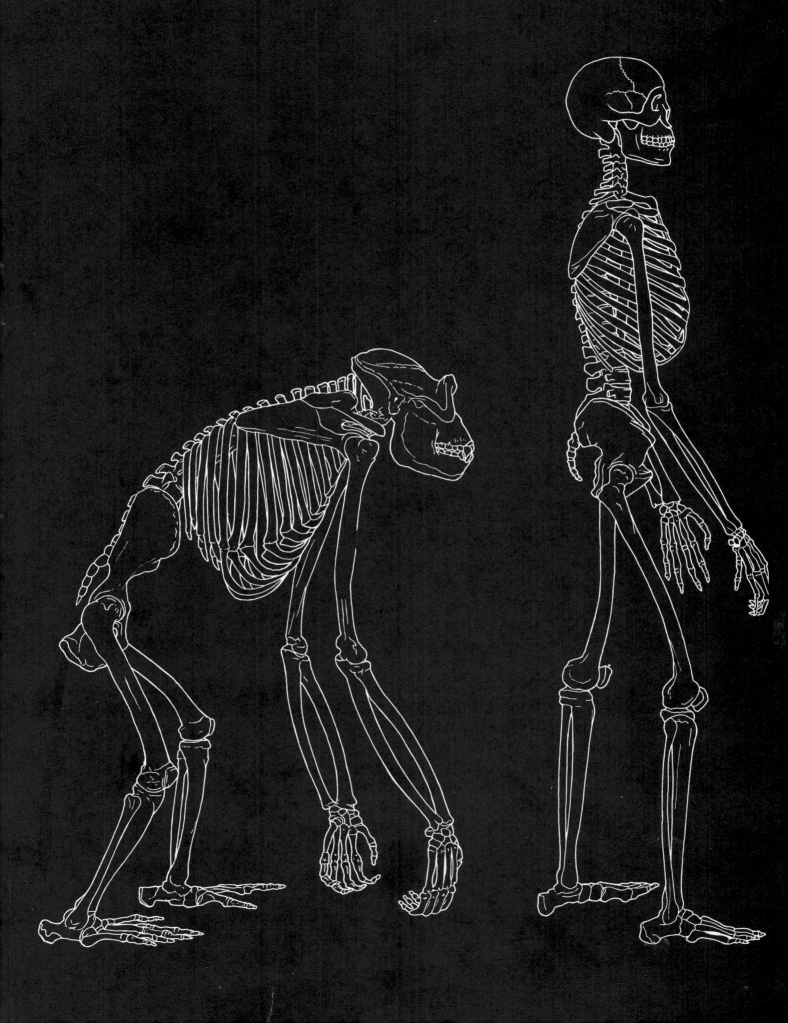

First published 1974
Macdonald and Co
(Publishers) Limited
St Giles House
49–50 Poland Street
London W1

© 1974 Macdonald and Co
(Publishers) Limited

Adapted by Tim Healey

Editor
Kate Woodhouse

Assistant Editor
Lesley Firth

Designer
Arthur Lockwood

Illustrators
Peter Connolly
Stephen Bennett
Linda Broad
Ray Burrows
Corinne Clarke
Ron Hayward
Anthony Morris
Tony Payne
John Smith
Jenny Thorne

Projects
Gillian Lockwood

Production
Philip Hughes

Published in the United
States by Silver Burdett
Company, Morristown, N.J.
1979 Printing
Library of Congress
Catalog Card No. 78-56603
ISBN 0-382-06188-8

The Life of
Monkeys
and Apes

Macdonald Educational

Lion-tailed macaque (monkey)

Chimpanzee (ape)

The Life of Monkeys and Apes

The names "monkey" and "ape"
do not have
exact meanings.
When we say "monkey"
we usually mean
climbers with short arms.
Almost all monkeys
have tails.
When we say "ape"
we usually mean
climbers with long arms.
Apes do not have tails.

Of all other animals,
monkeys and apes
look most like us.
There is a good reason.
Apes and humans come
from the same beginnings.
We come from the same
family of animals.
This family is called
"Primates."
"Primates" means the
first animals.

When we look at monkeys
or apes,
we see a strange version
of ourselves.
No wonder we laugh at them.
Maybe, we are really laughing
at ourselves.

Contents

How Primates Began

Changing shapes

The first primates came from the same beginnings
as some modern animals called "insectivores."
Insectivores means "insect eaters."
Shrews and moles are insectivores.
These animals lived in the ground.

When the first primates began to live in trees,
their fingers and toes got longer
so that they could hold onto branches.
Their eyes faced forward so they could see better
when they jumped from branch to branch.

Ring-tailed lemur

Tarsier

Bushbaby

Woolly monkey

Tree shrew

Prosimians
Prosimians are like
the very first primates.
Most of them are small.
They come out at night.

Tarsiers look like prosimians
and act like prosimians,
but they are more closely related
to monkeys.
Lemurs act rather like monkeys.

New World monkeys
These live in South America.
Marmosets climb like squirrels.
Bigger ones, such as woolly
monkeys, climb more like
Old World monkeys.

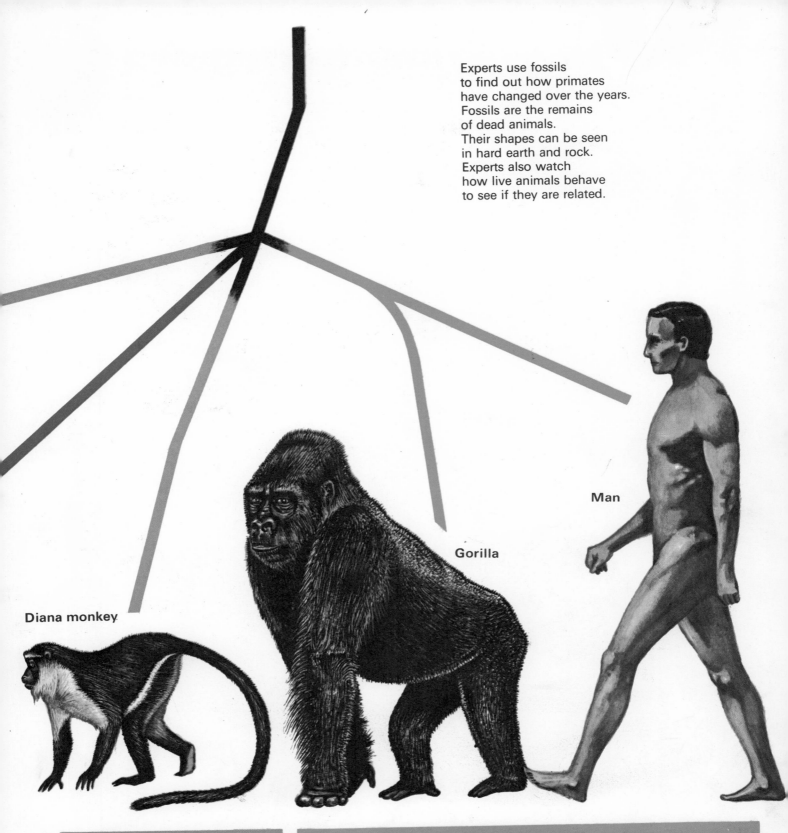

Experts use fossils
to find out how primates
have changed over the years.
Fossils are the remains
of dead animals.
Their shapes can be seen
in hard earth and rock.
Experts also watch
how live animals behave
to see if they are related.

Man

Gorilla

Diana monkey

Old World monkeys
Old World Monkeys live in
forests of Asia and Africa.
They have long tails.
Most live in troops.

Apes
Apes are more like humans
than any other primates.
They do not have tails.
They have long arms.

Humans
Humans have changed
more than any other primates
over millions of years.
We walk on our hind legs.

Close Relations

The ring-tailed lemur comes from Malagasy. It is active by day.

The ruffed lemur is a prosimian from Malagasy. Malagasy is a big island.

The aye-aye comes from Malagasy. It is a clumsy climber.

The tailless indris of Malagasy has strong hind legs.

The loris comes from the forests of southern Asia.

Tarsiers live in India
and the Philippines.
They look and act
a bit like bushbabies.

Bushbabies are good
nighttime climbers.
They live in the African
forests and bushlands.

The pottos of Africa
are very much like
the lorises of Asia,
but they have short tails.

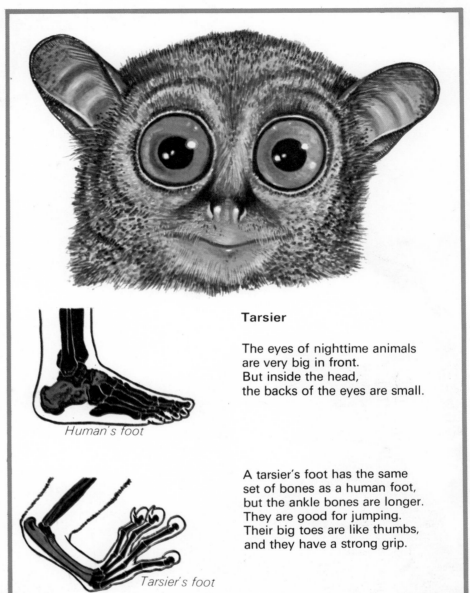

Human's foot

Tarsier's foot

Tarsier

The eyes of nighttime animals
are very big in front.
But inside the head,
the backs of the eyes are small.

A tarsier's foot has the same
set of bones as a human foot,
but the ankle bones are longer.
They are good for jumping.
Their big toes are like thumbs,
and they have a strong grip.

Prosimians

Humans, monkeys, and apes have some close relations.
These are some small climbing animals.
They come from hot parts of Africa and Asia.
They look a bit like the very first primates.
They are called "prosimians."
This means that they came before the monkeys.

Most prosimians spend their days sleeping in trees.
They wake up at night.
Their big eyes help them to see in the dark.
Some prosimians leap quickly from branch to branch.
Others move about more slowly.
They eat fruit, juicy leaves, and small animals.

11

Moving Around

Marmoset's hand

Marmosets are
the smallest monkeys.
They use their long nails to
dig into bark when they climb.

Macaque's hand

Monkeys and apes have thumbs
that go around branches
to give a good grip.
Their big toes do this, too.

Chimpanzee's hand

Monkeys and apes
use their hands to hold food
as humans do.
Their good grip is useful.

Arms, legs, and tails

Most apes and monkeys live among trees.
They have to be quite light to move among branches.
Heavy apes, such as gorillas,
and heavy monkeys, such as baboons,
spend much of their time on the ground.

Most monkeys climb on top of branches on four legs.
They have long tails.
They use their tails to keep balance.
Most apes swing underneath the branches.
They use only their arms.
This is one way to tell monkeys and apes apart.
But it is not always the rule.

Apes swing under the branches.
They often go hand over hand.
But sometimes they swing
from both arms at once.

Monkeys climb on top of
branches on four legs.
They use their long tails
to keep their balance.

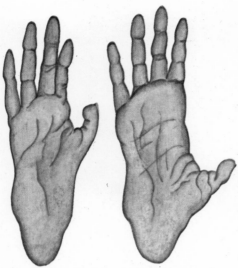

Macaque's foot   **Orangutan's foot**

These are the feet
of a macaque and an orangutan.
They both have long flat soles.
The big toes are like thumbs,
especially the orangutan's.

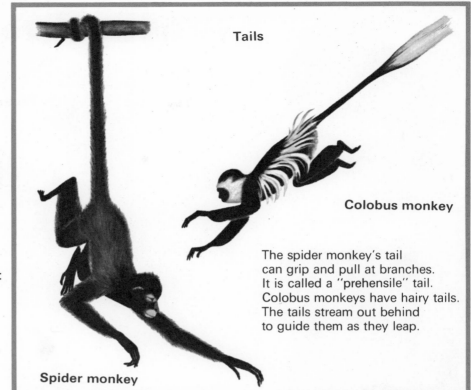

Tails

Colobus monkey

The spider monkey's tail
can grip and pull at branches.
It is called a "prehensile" tail.
Colobus monkeys have hairy tails.
The tails stream out behind
to guide them as they leap.

Spider monkey

Where Primates Live

Most primates live in or near
tropical forests.
The forests are hot
but there is plenty of rain, too.
Primary forests have tall trees.
Secondary forests are between
primary forests and grasslands.

Living space

Most primates have their favorite places to live.
Some like deep forests, others like grasslands.
They have their favorite types of food.
If there is not enough space or food in one place
they sometimes quarrel over it
with others of their kind.

Some primates live in troops.
Some troops have their own bit of land
called a "territory."
The troop sometimes defends its territory
against other troops of the same kind.

This picture shows
some African primates
at home:
1. red colobus
2. gorilla
3. de Brazza's monkey
4. white-collared
   mangabey
5. mandrill
6. grivet monkey
7. Guinea baboon.

Primary forest

Secondary forest

Clearing

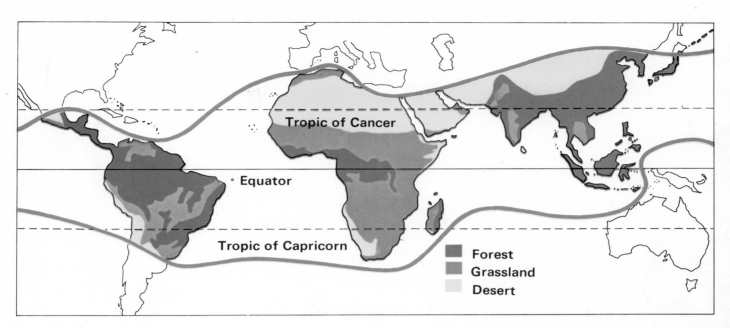

Tropic of Cancer

Equator

Tropic of Capricorn

Forest
Grassland
Desert

The parts of the world
between the red lines
are called the "tropics."
Most monkeys and apes
live in the tropics.

Howler monkeys

Groups of howler monkeys defend
their part of the forest
against other groups of howlers.
They howl to show the others
that this is their territory.

Secondary forest

Grassland

15

Senses

Nostrils of American monkeys point to the side.

Eyes and ears

There are five senses.
These are sight, smell, hearing, touch, and taste.

Monkeys and apes are like humans in many ways.
They have good eyesight.
They can see colors and tell how far away a thing is.
They also have good hearing and a good sense of touch.
But their sense of smell is poor.

The senses of monkeys and apes help them
to live their lives in the trees.
They need their good eyesight to leap for branches.
They need touch to feel for a good grip.
A good sense of smell is not as important to them.

Nostrils of monkeys from Africa and Asia point forward.

Apes, such as chimpanzees, have forward-pointing nostrils, also.

The hands of climbers have a good sense of touch.
Monkeys like to touch and hold each other.

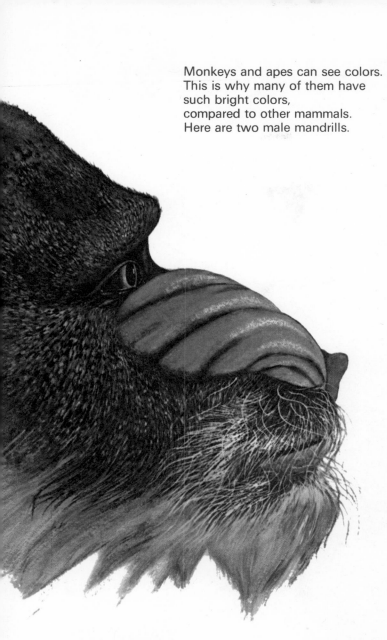

Monkeys and apes can see colors.
This is why many of them have
such bright colors,
compared to other mammals.
Here are two male mandrills.

The American douroucouli is
mainly active at night.
It has special eyes for
seeing in the dark.

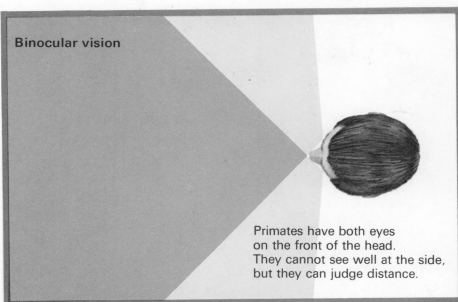

Binocular vision

Primates have both eyes
on the front of the head.
They cannot see well at the side,
but they can judge distance.

Looking for Food

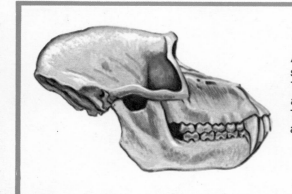

A baboon's teeth

Apes and monkeys have teeth
shaped like our own.
The long front teeth
are for biting and nibbling.
The back teeth
are for chewing.

Omnivores

Most animals prefer
either meat or plant food.
But many primates eat
a mixture of both.

Animals like this
are called "omnivores."
This word means
"eating plants and meat."
But it does not mean
that they do not care
what they eat.
Many primates are fussy.
Baboons like
the juiciest grass stems.
Orangutans love fruit
from the durian tree.

Monkeys and apes spend
much of their day
looking for food.
They usually eat plants.
Sometimes, they eat
insects, grubs, and
lizards as meat.
Some primates, such as
gorillas, never seem
to eat meat at all.

Apes and monkeys
use their hands for feeding.
This orangutan uses its feet
to hold the food, too.
The feet have a good grip.
Orangutans use their hands
to push back branches and leaves
when they look for food.

Different foods

	Fruit Flowers Nuts Seeds	Insects Grubs Lizards	Leaves Stems Roots Grasses
Chimpanzee	● ● ●	～～～	🍃
Macaque	● ● ●	～～	🍃
Capuchin	● ● ●	～～～	
Spider monkey	● ● ●		
Gorilla			🍃
Howler monkey			🍃

Most primates eat many kinds of food.
They like fruits and seeds, small animals,
and shoots and leaves.
Some primates are more fussy than others.
This chart shows the main foods they eat.

Some monkeys from Africa and Asia
can store food in their cheek pouches.
This Asian bonnet macaque has
filled its pouches with food
so it can have another meal later.

Gorillas look for food in troops
most often on the ground.
They like plant stems best.

Living Together

Family groups
Monkeys and apes
usually live in troops.
The troop keeps them
safe from enemies.
It gives company
for the young ones.
Some are family groups.
Then, two adults
guard the young ones.
The male and female
often look alike to us
in these family groups.

Titi monkeys of South America
live in family groups.
There are two adults
and up to three young ones.
The father helps to look after
the youngest baby.

Gibbons live in family groups
in forests of Southeast Asia.
There are two adults
and up to four young ones.

Male

Female

Bigger troops

Bigger troops often have
more females than males.
The males are often
bigger than the females.
They have brighter fur.
The strongest males
drive weaker males
away from the troop.
These outcasts make small
male troops of their own.
The males that stay
have ranks in the troop.
The strongest primate is the leader.

Gelada baboons live in troops
on the grassy hills of Ethiopia.
There is one adult male,
about six females, and many young.

Male

Female

Young one

Most monkeys and apes
live in troops that have
a few males, about twice
as many females, and about
four times as many young ones.
These are Japanese macaques.

Female

Male

Macaque threat

Fixed stare

Open mouth

Head bobbing

When a macaque feels fierce,
it stares. Then, it shows its teeth,
while bobbing its head up and down.

Language

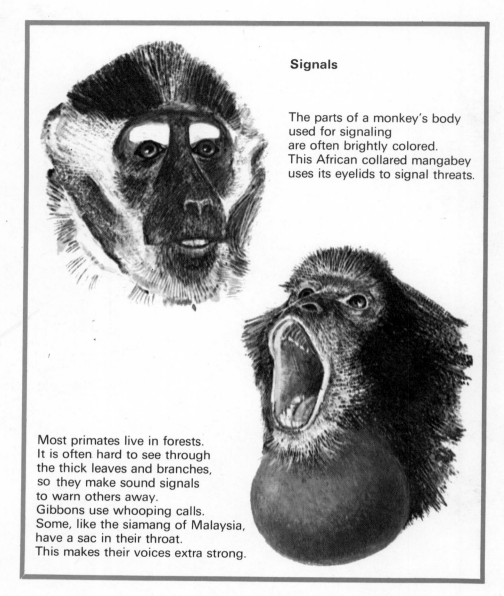

Signals

The parts of a monkey's body
used for signaling
are often brightly colored.
This African collared mangabey
uses its eyelids to signal threats.

Most primates live in forests.
It is often hard to see through
the thick leaves and branches,
so they make sound signals
to warn others away.
Gibbons use whooping calls.
Some, like the siamang of Malaysia,
have a sac in their throat.
This makes their voices extra strong.

Monkeys have ranks in their troops.
The pig tailed macaque on the left walks boldly.
The one on the right is not as important.

Signals

There are two kinds of
language.
There are words
and signals.
Humans use both kinds.

Words have to be learned.
You would not understand
someone who spoke
Japanese words.
But you would understand
if they laughed or cried.
This sort of language
is born in you.
You are using signals.

Monkeys and apes
do not use words,
but they do use signals.
They have their own way
of showing their feelings.
They make certain noises
and faces.
These are not the same
as human noises and faces.
Monkeys of Africa and Asia
smack their lips quickly.
This means the same thing
as a human smile.

Gorillas usually go on all fours on the ground.
If angry, they stand up and beat their chests.
This is a sign of warning. It means "watch out."
A warning is often enough. They rarely fight.

Chimpanzee expressions

Alert   **Happy**   **Afraid**   **Excited**

Chimpanzees make faces to show their moods.

23

Attack and Defense

Leopards eat monkeys and apes
if they get the chance.
Troops of chimps sometimes
use branches to drive them off.

Wild hunting dogs are fierce.
It is the job of male baboons
to defend the baboon troops.
They have strong, sharp teeth.

Enemies

Wild animals face danger
from enemies all the time.
This is why it is good
to be part of a troop.
Then, the whole troop can
look out for danger.

Monkeys and apes
usually climb up trees
if they are scared.
Once they are up safely,
they chatter at the enemy.
Some throw dead branches.

But some enemies can
reach them in the trees.
Eagles can swoop down.
Leopards can climb up.

If there is no escape
the whole troop
faces the enemy together.
Monkeys and apes have
sharp teeth.
Big males can be fierce.
It is the young ones
who face the most danger.

Many enemies cannot climb trees.
Monkeys and apes sleep in trees
for safety at night,
even if they live on the ground
in the day.

Enemies

Crowned hawk eagle

The African crowned hawk eagle
sometimes snatches the young.
The South American anaconda
can swallow monkeys whole.

Anaconda

Birth

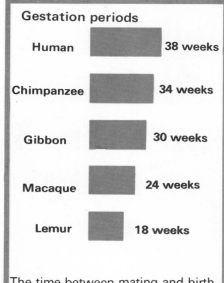

Gestation periods

Human	38 weeks
Chimpanzee	34 weeks
Gibbon	30 weeks
Macaque	24 weeks
Lemur	18 weeks

The time between mating and birth is called the "gestation period." The animal grows in the mother during this time.

Patas monkey

Monkeys groom each other to show that they are friends. They are not looking for fleas. They rarely have them. They just enjoy making a fuss over one another.

Spectacled langur

Birth often takes place at night. The baby is born head first. The mother bites through the cord that joins them. Then she cleans the baby and starts to give it milk.

Babies

Most female primates
can only mate
and have their babies
at certain times
of the year.
The babies are born
when there is
plenty of food.

Some female monkeys
from Africa and Asia
grow colored lumps
on their buttocks.
These are signals
for the males,
which show that
mating time has come.

Most monkeys and apes
have only one baby
at a time.
The baby clings
to its mother
with its tiny hands.
As it gets bigger
it leaves
the mother's breast.
It sometimes
rides on her back.

Macaque

A baby primate
clings to its mother's breast.
She takes the baby with her
wherever she goes.

Common marmoset

Marmosets often have twins
and sometimes triplets.
They are the only primates
that do this.
The others have their babies
one at a time.

27

Childhood

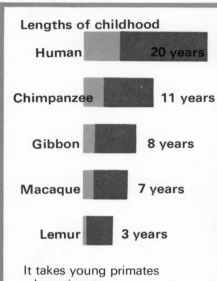

Lengths of childhood

Human — 20 years

Chimpanzee — 11 years

Gibbon — 8 years

Macaque — 7 years

Lemur — 3 years

It takes young primates
a long time to grow up.
The orange shapes on this chart
show babyhood.
The brown shows childhood.

These are Asian langurs.
Mother monkeys in big troops
are not jealous.
They let other mothers
handle their babies
and groom them.

Mother chimpanzees
play with their babies
just as a human mother
plays with her child.

Young chimpanzees learn
from adults.
This young one learns how
to get termites from a nest.

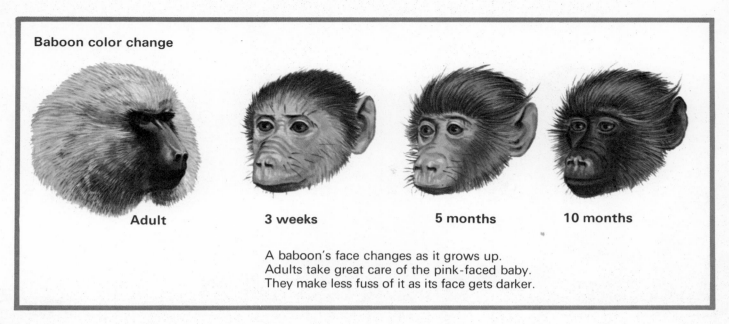

Baboon color change

Adult   3 weeks   5 months   10 months

A baboon's face changes as it grows up.
Adults take great care of the pink-faced baby.
They make less fuss of it as its face gets darker.

Play

Mother monkeys and
apes watch their babies
with care at first.
Then the babies start
to move about
on their own.
This is when
they start to play.

Play is important.
The young ones learn
how to run and climb.
They explore.
They learn how to fight.
Sometimes they make
special faces for play.
The faces show
they are playing games.

The young ones learn how to get
along with others when they play.
They also watch the adults carefully.
They copy the things that adults do,
and learn in this way, too.

Young chimpanzees play with others
of the same age.
The play can look rough,
but they rarely hurt each other.

Intelligence

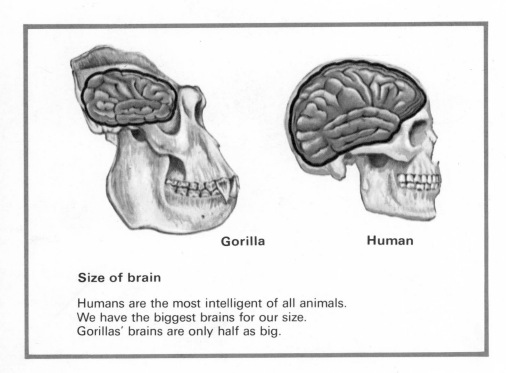

Gorilla   **Human**

Size of brain

Humans are the most intelligent of all animals.
We have the biggest brains for our size.
Gorillas' brains are only half as big.

Intelligent animals can adapt.
They can change their ways
to suit their surroundings.
Indian rhesus monkeys
have learned to look for
food and scraps in towns.

Instinct

Animals behave
in two main ways.
They behave by instinct
and by intelligence.

Most animals use instinct
a lot of the time.
Instinct is born in them.
They do not have to learn it.
Monkeys and apes
do not have to learn
how to suck milk
when they are young,
for example.
This is an instinct.

Intelligence

But primates behave
in another way, too.
They use intelligence.
When something happens
they learn from it.
They may behave
in a new way
if it happens again.
They store away facts
in their memories.
The facts may be useful
later on.

Monkeys, apes,
and humans
go on learning
all their lives.
But they learn fastest
when they are young.

This chimpanzee learns
to pile up the boxes
so he can reach the fruit.

This chimpanzee solves
a tricky problem
to win a reward.

Monkeys in zoos

Monkeys and apes get used
to living in zoos
more than other animals.
This is because they can adapt.

American Monkeys

The common marmoset and its closest relations have tufts of hair on their ears. The golden lion marmoset is really a tamarin.

Common marmoset

Golden lion marmoset

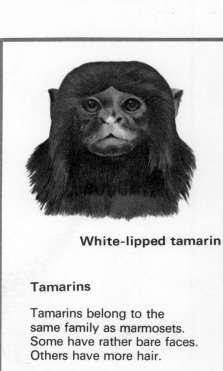

White-lipped tamarin

Tamarins

Tamarins belong to the same family as marmosets. Some have rather bare faces. Others have more hair.

Emperor tamarin

Monkeys of the forest

The forests of Central America and South America are very big indeed. They hold many monkeys. There are so many monkeys that no one has sorted out all of the kinds yet.

The smallest are called marmosets. They have nails like claws instead of flat fingernails. True marmosets have tails marked with dark rings.

Tamarins are a bit bigger than marmosets. But they are close relations. Marmosets and tamarins live in family groups. But they sometimes join troops of bigger monkeys. Woolly monkeys, spider monkeys, and capuchins are some of these bigger monkeys. They have toes that can grip branches.

Saki

Saki monkeys live
all around the Amazon.
They are good climbers.

Squirrel monkey

Squirrel monkeys like
the riverside forests
of the Amazon River.
They live in big troops.

Red uakari

Red uakaris live
in the deep forests
of western Brazil.
Sometimes they swing
on their arms like apes.

Woolly monkey

Woolly monkeys, spider monkeys,
and capuchins
can cling with their tails.
The woolly monkey is
the biggest American monkey.
The spider monkey is
a very good acrobat.
Capuchins live in big troops.
They mix with other monkeys.

Capuchin

Spider monkey

Monkeys of Africa and Asia

White-collared mangabey

Owl-faced guenon

Drill

Barbary ape

These are all monkeys
of Africa and Asia.
They come in many shapes
and sizes.

Black ape

Hamadryas baboon

Red colobus

The red colobus of Africa
and the golden langur of Asia
are leaf-eating monkeys.

Golden langur

The proboscis monkey is a leaf-eater
from the forests of Borneo.
Only the male has a big nose.

Colorful monkeys

Most monkeys of Africa
and Asia eat insects
as well as plant food.
They have cheek pouches.

In Africa,
guenons and mangabeys
live in the trees.
They are the best climbers.
Drills and mandrills
live on the forest floor.
Baboons live among rocks
or in grasslands.

In Asia,
macaques live on the ground.
There are some macaques
called "barbary apes."
They have no tails.
They are called apes, but
they are really monkeys.
They live in Africa, too.

Leaf-eating monkeys
have no cheek pouches.
The colobus of Africa
and langurs of Asia
are leaf-eating monkeys.

Proboscis monkey

The Baboon Troop

Life in the troop
There can be 20 or 30 baboons in a troop.
But some troops have up to 80 baboons.
Each troop has its own bit of land called the "home range."
Baboons sleep in trees in the middle of their range.

At dawn, they go off to look for food on the plains.
Baboons must drink once a day at a water hole.
Sometimes they meet other troops here.
Cheetahs, wild dogs, and leopards are enemies.
It takes young baboons five years to grow up.
They may live for 20 years, if they are lucky.

Africa

Arabia

Baboons

Baboons live in the grasslands
of many parts of Africa.
There are many kinds of baboons.

Gnu

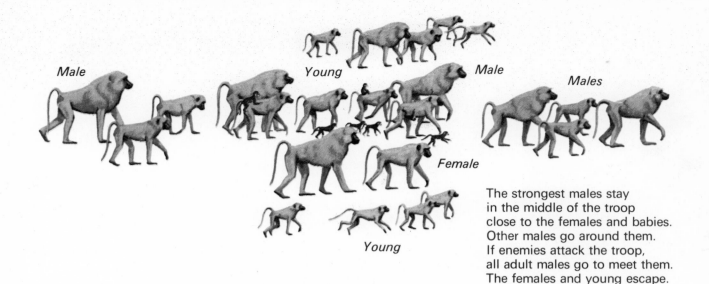

Male

Young

Male

Males

Female

Young

The strongest males stay
in the middle of the troop
close to the females and babies.
Other males go around them.
If enemies attack the troop,
all adult males go to meet them.
The females and young escape.

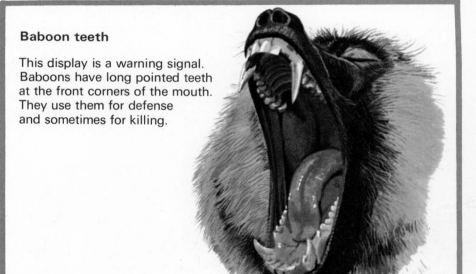

Baboon teeth

This display is a warning signal.
Baboons have long pointed teeth
at the front corners of the mouth.
They use them for defense
and sometimes for killing.

Baboons spend much of the day
looking for food.
Sometimes they rest
and groom each other.
The strongest males always
get their own way in the troop.
They are the fathers
of most of the babies.

Zebra

Impala

Gibbons

Concolor gibbon

Capped gibbon

Hoolock gibbon

Lar gibbon

Siamang

Southeast Asia

Good climbers

Gibbons are very good climbers.
They spend most of their time in trees.
All day long, they make loud sounds
to defend their territory.
They live in small family groups.
At night, the family huddles together.
In daytime, they search for fruit, leaves, and buds.
They sometimes eat insects and small birds, too.

There are many kinds of gibbons.
They live in the forests
of Southeast Asia.

Gibbons swing hand over hand
under the branches
when they are in a hurry.
They have long arms.
These take them a long way.
They can also swing
from both arms at once.

Walking upright

Gibbons walk upright
on the ground.

Orangutans

Orangutans are apes that feed mostly on fruit.
Sometimes they live in small family groups.
Sometimes they live on their own.
They make a nest of branches each night.
They cover themselves with big leaves in wet weather.
Orangutans can live for about 40 years.

Sumatra
Borneo

■ Orangutan

Orangutans live in Sumatra
and Borneo.
They like low, swampy forests.

Male orangutans are much bigger
than the females.
The males have wide cheek pads.
Orangutans climb on thick branches
among the trees.
They hardly ever come down
to the ground.

Male orangutan

Morgan Hill
Country School

A Chimpanzee's Day

Africa

☐ Chimpanzee

☐ Pygmy chimpanzee

Chimpanzees live in the forests of central and west Africa. There are two kinds.

Food

Chimpanzees make leafy beds to sleep in.
At dawn, they wake and go off to look for food.
They eat mainly plant food, which is not very filling,
so they need many meals during the day.
When a chimpanzee finds food, he drums and hoots,
so that the rest of the band can come and share it.
Some chimpanzees eat the meat of animals,
such as small antelopes and monkeys.

The chimpanzees rest from time to time.
They groom each other, while the young ones play.
They have their own special friends, just like us.

Walking on the ground

Chimpanzees walk on all fours most of the time. The knuckles of their hands just touch the ground. They can stand up, also.

Drinking water

Chimpanzees are very intelligent.
They can use simple tools.
This chimpanzee is making a
sponge out of leaves,
so he can drink water.

Chimpanzees like company
but they do not live in real troops.
Some wander off and join
other bands of chimpanzees
for a while.

Each chimpanzee makes a bed
high in a tree, every night.
It bends branches together
and covers them with leaves.

The Shy Gorillas

Lowland
gorilla

Mountain
gorilla

Most gorillas live
in the thick forests of
Africa.
But some rare gorillas
live on mountain slopes.

Heavy apes

Gorillas are by far the heaviest apes.
They are quiet and peaceful most of the time.
Gorillas are shy.
They do not groom each other or play as much
as chimpanzees.

They eat only plant food, such as leaves and shoots.
They have strong jaws to bite through the shoots.
The male gorilla leads the troop
when they search for food in the forest.
He is the first to make his bed in the evening.
Gorillas can live for 30 or 40 years.
They have no real enemies, apart from humans.

Gorillas live in troops.
But for much of the time
they do not seem
to notice each other.
There are 15 or 16 gorillas in a
troop. There is only one male.
He is bigger than the females,
and has a silvery back.

Female gorillas make nests
high up in the trees.
The heavy male makes his nest
on the ground or near it.

Threat display

Hooting

Fake feeding

Throwing
branches

Chest beating

Running
sideways

Ground
thumping

Male gorillas are very strong,
but they are peaceful
for most of the time.
When danger comes,
they make a threat display.
They do the things shown above.
This display is enough
to frighten off most attackers.

Cousins

We find out about
the first humans from fossils.
The first human fossils
came from Africa.
Experts dug them up
and put them together.

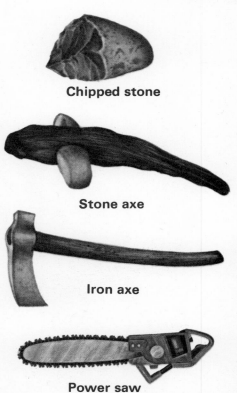

Chipped stone

Stone axe

Iron axe

Power saw

Humans used intelligence
to make all sorts of tools.
The first humans used chipped stone
for cutting, for example.
Then humans made axes.
Now we use power saws.

Australopithecus

Australopithecus was an ape man.
He lived in Africa
about two million years ago.
Experts found bits of skull.
They put them together
to find out what he looked like.
He was shorter than modern man,
but he walked upright.

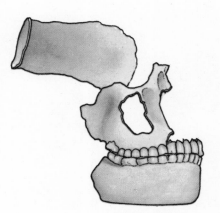

Bits of skull

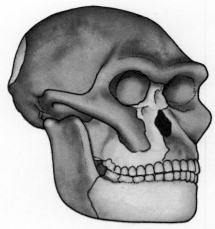

Model of skull

Young people love
to climb and play
just as other young primates do.

Artist's picture of Australopithecus

Cousins

Humans do not come from apes.
But we come from the same beginnings.
We are like cousins.

Long ago, our first ancestors
walked on all fours, a bit like gorillas.
Bit by bit, they came to walk on two legs.
This left their hands free to hold things.
They had bigger brains than other animals.
They learned to use simple tools.
Very slowly, their brains grew larger.
They learned to use words as well as signals.
Finally, they became human.

People and Primates

Barbary ape

Hapi was a god
of the Ancient Egyptians.
He had the body of a man
and the head of a baboon.

Hanuman was a monkey
in the Hindu religion.
He was a friend of the god Rama.
He fought by Rama's side.

Barbary apes are really macaques.
Macaques are monkeys.
Some live in Gibraltar.
British troops came to rule
Gibraltar in 1704.
A tale says that when
the barbary apes leave Gibraltar
the British will leave too.

First drawing
The first European drawing
of an ape was made
just over 300 years ago.
The artist made the ape look
very much like a human.

Charles Darwin
Charles Darwin found out
that different animals come
from the same beginnings.
People made fun of him at first.
They thought he meant
that humans came from monkeys.

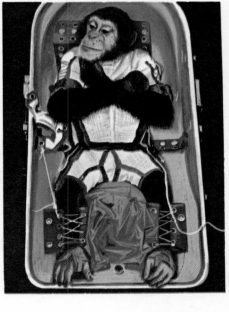

Men or monsters

Monkeys and apes
look very much like
strange sorts of humans.
For thousands of years
people imagined
strange things about them.

Some people thought
they were gods.
Others thought
they were monsters.
Some thought apes
were wild men.
"Orangutan" means
old man of the woods.

We have only found out
about monkeys and apes
recently.
Charles Darwin found out
that monkeys and apes
come from the same
beginnings as humans.
Then people watched them
in the wild to find out
how they really lived.

Monkeys look very much
like funny kinds of humans.
People used them as performers
for this reason.
Organ grinders often used them
to catch people's attention.
They often used capuchins.

Monkeys and apes have bodies
very much like human bodies.
People use them for tests
for this reason.
Before men went into space
they sent up chimpanzees
to find out if they could live there.

Today, we know that
most gorillas are shy.
But we like to think of them
as savage monsters.
This is King Kong.

The Threat to Primates

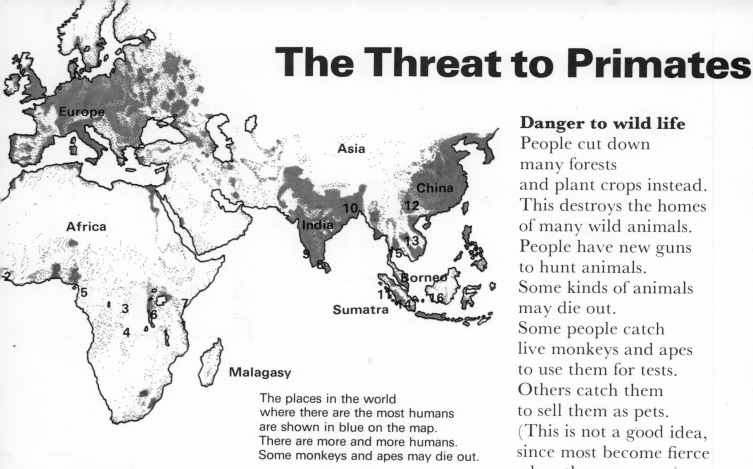

The numbers show the homes
of the rarest monkeys and apes
of Africa and Asia.

1. red colobus of Zanzibar
2. olive colobus
3. chimpanzee
4. pygmy chimpanzee
5. lowland gorilla
6. mountain gorilla
7. Tana river mangabey and
   Tana red colobus

8. lion-tailed macaque
9. John's langur
10. golden langur
11. pig tailed langur
12. snubnosed langur
13. douc langur
14. Kloss's gibbon
15. pileated gibbon
16. orangutan

Malagasy

The places in the world
where there are the most humans
are shown in blue on the map.
There are more and more humans.
Some monkeys and apes may die out.

Danger to wild life

People cut down
many forests
and plant crops instead.
This destroys the homes
of many wild animals.
People have new guns
to hunt animals.
Some kinds of animals
may die out.
Some people catch
live monkeys and apes
to use them for tests.
Others catch them
to sell them as pets.
(This is not a good idea,
since most become fierce
when they grow up.)

But others have seen
the danger to wild life.
They have made parks
and forests
where animals can live.
No one can harm them here.

People catch many wild monkeys
and send them away for tests.
Today there are laws to protect
rare species in many lands.

Classification

"Classification" means dividing animals up into groups. The main groups are called "families." The smaller groups in each family are called "species." Experts sometimes have different ideas about which group primates belong to. This is just one way to classify them.

The marmoset family

Marmosets live in Central and South America. They are a type of monkey. Tamarins are related to marmosets. There are about 30 species of marmosets and tamarins.

The true American monkey family

There are about 35 other species of monkeys in Central and South America. They are true monkeys.

Old World monkeys

"Old World monkeys" means monkeys of Asia and Africa. There are 37 species that eat a mixture of meat and plant food. These are:

macaques (13 species) Most live in Asia. Barbary apes, black apes, and rhesus monkeys are all macaques.

In Africa there are: guenons (11 species) baboons (5 species) mangabeys (4 species) drill mandrill patas monkey gelada

Old World leaf-eating monkeys

There are 23 species: leaf monkey (15 species) snub-nosed monkey (2 species) colobus monkey (4 species) proboscis monkey, langur

The gibbon family

Gibbons live in forests of Southeast Asia. They are small apes. There are 7 species: the lar, agile, silvery, hoolock, black, and dwarf gibbons, and the siamang.

The great ape family

There are 5 species: orangutan chimpanzee pygmy chimpanzee lowland gorilla mountain gorilla

Facts and Figures

Mammals

Primates are mammals.
This means that
the mothers
feed the young ones
on their own milk.

There are 18 groups
of mammals.
Primates are one of
the biggest groups.
But most monkeys and apes
live in the tropics.
So there are many parts
of the world
where the only primates
are humans.

Common and rare

It is hard to know
which monkeys and apes
are the most common, and
which are the most rare.
The howler monkeys
of South America
may be the most common.
The golden lion marmosets
of South America
may be the most rare.

Brains

Apes are more intelligent
than monkeys, on the whole.
These are average sizes
of the brains
of apes and humans:

Gibbon	100 ccs (3.5 oz)
Orangutan	375 ccs (13 oz)
Chimpanzee	365 ccs (13 oz)
Gorilla	490 ccs (17 oz)
Human	1390 ccs (49 oz)

Gorillas have
the biggest brains
of all the apes.
Does this mean
that they are cleverest?
Maybe, but
we cannot be sure.
It is hard to get
adult gorillas
to take tests
to find out.

Biggest and smallest

The smallest monkey
is the pygmy marmoset
of South America.
It is about
300 mm (12 ins) long.
It weighs 60 grams (2 oz).
The biggest ape
is the lowland gorilla
of Africa.
It is about
1720 mm (5.5 ft) tall.
It weighs 180 kilograms (397 lbs).

The oldest

We know very little
about how long
monkeys and apes
live in the wild.
We cannot follow them
from birth to death
to find out
how long they live.
But we can tell
some things from
animals in zoos.

Zoo animals
probably live longer
than wild ones.
They are not hunted,
and get plenty of food.
Vets look after them
when they are ill.

One chimpanzee lived
for about 50 years
in an American zoo.
He holds the record
for long life.

Male gorilla

Pygmy marmoset

Important Words

Ape
In this book,
the word "ape" means
a primate with long arms
and with no tail.
The true apes are the gorillas,
orangutans, chimpanzees,
and gibbons.
Some monkeys have short tails
or no tails at all,
such as the barbary ape
and the black ape.
They are called "apes" but
they are really monkeys.

Binocular vision
This means
seeing the same thing
with both eyes at once.
To do this well, an animal needs
both eyes at the front of its head.
Monkeys and apes have this vision.
It helps them to judge distance.

Cheek pouches
These are pouches
in the cheeks of some animals.
They can store and carry food
in their cheek pouches.
They can eat the food later.

Dominant males
These are the biggest
and strongest males
in a troop of monkeys.

Family
This word has
two different meanings.
It can just mean mother,
father, and the young ones.
It can also mean
a whole group of primates
such as the gibbon family.
This sort of family may be made
up of many different species.

Fossil
A fossil is the remains
of a dead animal
buried in the earth.
Most fossils are made up of
the hardest parts of the body,
such as teeth and bones.
They turn to stone in time.
Other traces of animals of long ago
such as footprints, for example,
can be fossils, too.

Gestation period
This is the time
between the mating of animals
and the birth of the baby.
During this time, the animal
grows inside its mother.

Home range
Some animals roam over
one area of land all their lives.
This is the "home range."
It is not the same as "territory."
Groups of animals may share it
with others of their kind.

Insectivores
This word can mean
all animals which eat insects.
It can also mean a certain group
of small animals, such as
shrews, moles, and hedgehogs.
Primates may come from the same
beginnings as these insectivores.

Instinct
An instinct is
any kind of behavior
that animals know from birth.
They do not have to learn it.

Intelligence
This means
learning facts
and putting them together
to solve a problem.
It is a rare kind of behavior
in most animals.
Monkeys and apes are intelligent.
Humans are the most intelligent
animals that have ever lived.

Mammal
This is the name for one
of the main kinds of animals.
Mammals have a backbone.
They have some hair or fur.
They have warm blood.
They are fed on milk
when they are babies.
Primates are mammals.

Monkey
In this book,
"monkey" means a primate
with arms and legs
of about the same size.
Most monkeys have long tails.

New World
This means America.

Old World
This means
Europe, Africa, and Asia.
The only primates in Europe,
apart from humans,
are barbary apes of Gibraltar.

Omnivores
These are animals
that eat both plant food
(such as fruit and leaves)
and animal food
(such as meat and eggs).

Prehensile
This word means
being able to grip.
Monkeys and apes have
prehensile toes and fingers.
Some monkeys of South America
have prehensile tails.
These are the spider monkeys,
howler monkeys, woolly monkeys,
and capuchins.

Primates
This is the name
of a group of mammals.
They are the first group.
Humans, monkeys, apes, and
prosimians are all primates.

Prosimians
These are one kind
of primate.
Tree shrews, lemurs, pottos, and
bush babies are all prosimians.
Prosimians means
"the ones that came before
the monkeys and apes."
Of all the primates,
they have changed the least
over the years.

Territory
This is a bit of land
which one animal
or one group of animals
think of as their own.
They defend it against
others of their species.
Gibbons have territories,
for example.

Troop
This is the name for
a band of monkeys or apes
who live together
in the same territory.

Making a Chimpanzee

You will need:
2 card centers from paper towels
2 card centers from toilet paper
1 small washing up liquid bottle
1 soft margarine tub (1 lb size)
1 plastic, round, half-gallon
  ice cream container
1 egg box
thin card (from cereal packet)
2 black buttons, thick string,
sticky tape, newspaper

Rub the tubs and bottle with
sandpaper, so the paint will stick.
Stuff the tubes with newspaper.
Pleat one end of each tube, and
tape to hold the pleat together.

Put the top of the margarine tub
on the thin card and draw round it.
Add ears and cut out the shape.

Stuff the two tubs with newspaper.
Tape the card to the margarine tub.
Tape the ice cream container to
the other side of the card shape.

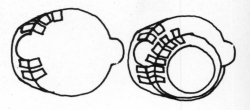

Cut a hole in the margarine tub
so the neck of the bottle
can fit into it.

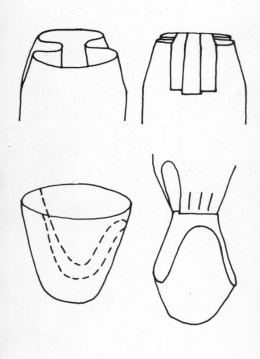

Cut hands and feet from
the cups of the egg box.

Pleat the other ends
of the four tubes.
Fit in a hand or foot to each.
Tape or staple to fix.

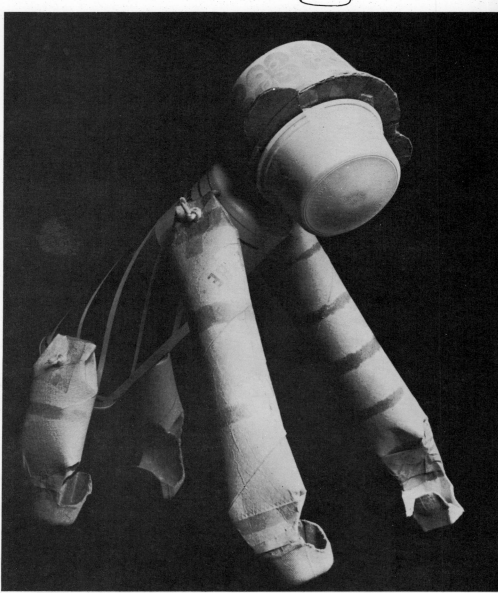

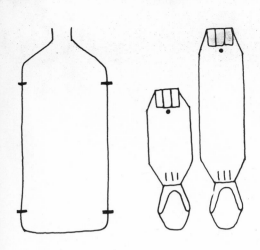

Make holes with a needle
in the bottle, and in
the tops of the arms and legs.
Thread the needle with some string.
Tie a knot to one end of the string.
Thread through one arm, then
through the holes in the bottle
through the other arm. Knot it.
Do the same for the legs.
Press on the head.

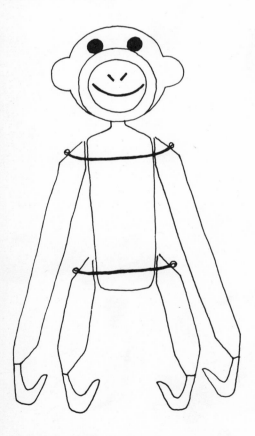

Paint all surfaces except for
the face and insides of the hands
with thick brown poster paint.
Paint the face and insides of hands
with light brown poster paint.
Stick on buttons for eyes.
Paint on the mouth and nose.

Making a Gorilla

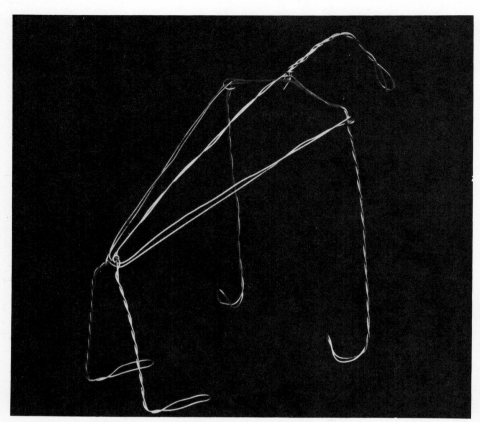

You will need:
Wire—strong but easy to bend
Newspaper and paper paste
Buttons or beads for the eyes

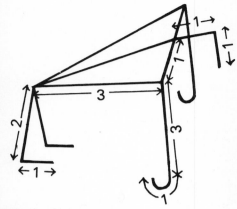

Bend the wire into a frame
as shown in the picture.
The measurements can be
in inches or centimeters.

Tear a large newspaper
into four long strips.
Tear a small one into two strips.
Roll each strip into a spill.
Dab the ends with glue to hold.

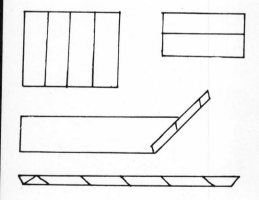

Wind the arms and legs of the frame
with many layers of spills.
Fasten the endings with sticky tape.
Screw a sheet of newspaper
into a sausage shape.
Fit it under the body with tape.
Wind the head and body with spills.
Make strong shoulders and
a thick neck.

Mix up some paper paste.
Tear some more newspaper
into small strips.
Damp the strips with paste
and cover the gorilla with
a double layer.
Screw small pieces of newspaper
into flat balls for muscles.
Look at the pictures of gorillas
in this book.
See where the bones and muscles go.

Let the model dry.
Paint it with poster paint.
Glue on beads or buttons for eyes.

Going to the Zoo

A family of gibbons

Draw to remember
The best way
to remember details
is to draw them.
All you need is
a pencil and
a pad of paper.
If you want to make
colored pictures,
draw outlines for
the colored areas.
Make a note of
the colors.
Do the painting later,
when you get home.

Watch one group
It costs a lot
of time and money
to watch monkeys
and apes
in the wild.
But you can see
them in a zoo.

Some people move from
one cage to another.
They want to see
everything at once.
They end up
hot and tired.

It is much better
to spend a long time
just watching
one group.
Then you see more
than just what
animals look like.
You see them behave.

Look carefully
Choose one animal.
Look at it carefully.
Start with the head.
Then look slowly
at the body.
Look at the markings
on the skin and fur.
Look at hands and feet.
Don't forget to look
at the big toe.
If it has a tail,
watch how it carries it.
Then close your eyes.
See if you can remember
what you have seen.

It does not matter if
you are not a good artist.
It is still worth doing.
Drawing helps you
to remember details.
If you find it too hard to
draw the whole animal,
try drawing parts,
such as the face,
hands, and feet.

Geladas grooming each other

A male baboon threatening a female baboon

Living in groups

Monkeys and apes like company.
There is usually more than one monkey
in each cage at the zoo.
How many there are depends on the species.

There are never more than two adult gibbons
in a cage, because the males
do not get along with other adult males.
The females dislike other females.

In bigger troops, there may be many adult females,
but there is only one adult male.
Adult males can keep out of each other's way
in the wild
but there could be fights in the cages.

Most adult male monkeys and apes
are bigger than the adult females.
They have brighter markings.
Sort out males, females, and young ones.
Watch how they behave.
Who seems to be the boss? Who comes second?
Are the young ones rude or well-behaved?

Signals

Look at pages 22–23.
Try to remember
friendly signals
and threat signals
when you go to zoos.
Remember that
when monkeys groom
each other,
they show that
they are friends.
The bossy ones
are groomed
more than
they groom the others.

Once you think
you understand
monkey signals
you can use them.
Try smacking
your lips quickly
with Old World
monkeys,
for example.
Remember that this
is a sort of smile.
How do they behave
when you do this?

An orangutan choosing its food

Going to Museums

Museums

You can have fun
and learn a lot
about monkeys
and apes
in a museum.
As in the zoo,
it is better
to look closely
at a few things
than to try
to see all there is.
Take your pencil,
a pad of paper,
and an eraser.

Drawing

Stuffed monkeys
and apes are
easier to draw
than live ones.
They do not move about.
Make yourself
comfortable.
Take your time
and do your best.
Use a soft pencil
but make sure
the point is sharp.
Sketch the main lines
softly at first.
Then add details.
You can
rub them out if
you make a mistake.
Make big drawings.
These give more space
for details.

Looking at bones

The humps and hollows on bones all have a job to do.
The big bumps and flat parts, for example,
are the places where muscles join the bones.
Muscles cause movement.
Put your fingers on the side of your forehead.
Clench and unclench your teeth a few times.
You can feel your jaw muscles moving.
Muscles go up from the jaw to the forehead.
Male gorillas have bigger jaw muscles.
They go right up to the top of the head
and join on to a ridge there.

Most mammals have similar sets of bones.
But they come in different shapes and sizes.
Horses have short thighs, for example,
so their knees are rather high up.
They walk on tiptoe. The hoof is a toenail.
Looking at bones can help you to draw.
The skeleton shows exactly where joints are.
It shows where an animal can and cannot bend.

Fossils

Fossils are shapes
of plants and animals
kept for ages
in the earth.
The earth hardens.
The shape is left.
Some museums have
fossils of ape men
and early men.
These fossils
are very rare.
But many museums
have models of them
even if they don't have
the fossils themselves.

Gorilla's skull

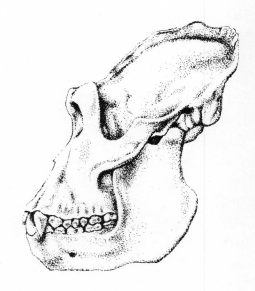

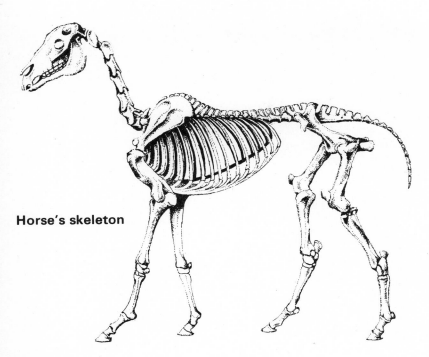
Horse's skeleton

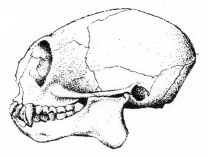
Marmoset's skull

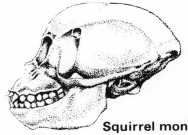
Squirrel monkey's skull

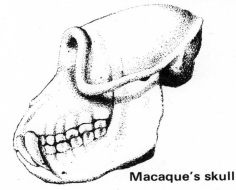
Macaque's skull

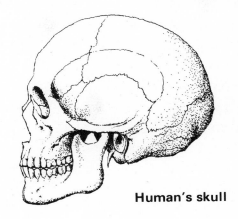
Chimpanzee's skull

Human's skull

Teeth

You can see the teeth of animals better
in a museum than in the wild.
Mammals have four main kinds of teeth.
Incisors are the flat front teeth.
Canines are in the corner of the mouth.
They are pointed like fangs.
Premolars come behind the canines.
Primates use them for chewing.
They have bumpy tops.
Molars are at the back of the mouth.
They are large chewing teeth.
They have bumpy tops, too.

Skeletons

Monkeys, apes, and humans all have
the same number of vertebrae.
These are joints of the backbone and neck.
Each vertebra has a pair of ribs
in the area around the chest.
Count the number of vertebrae in this part
of the body.
See if all primates are alike.
Of course, apes do not have proper tails,
while monkeys have more vertebrae.
But apes and humans do have
some tail vertebrae.
It is worth counting.

Index

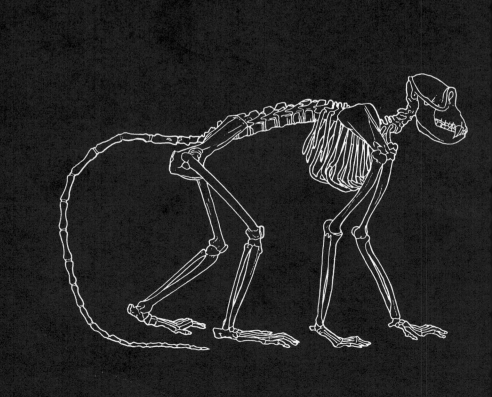

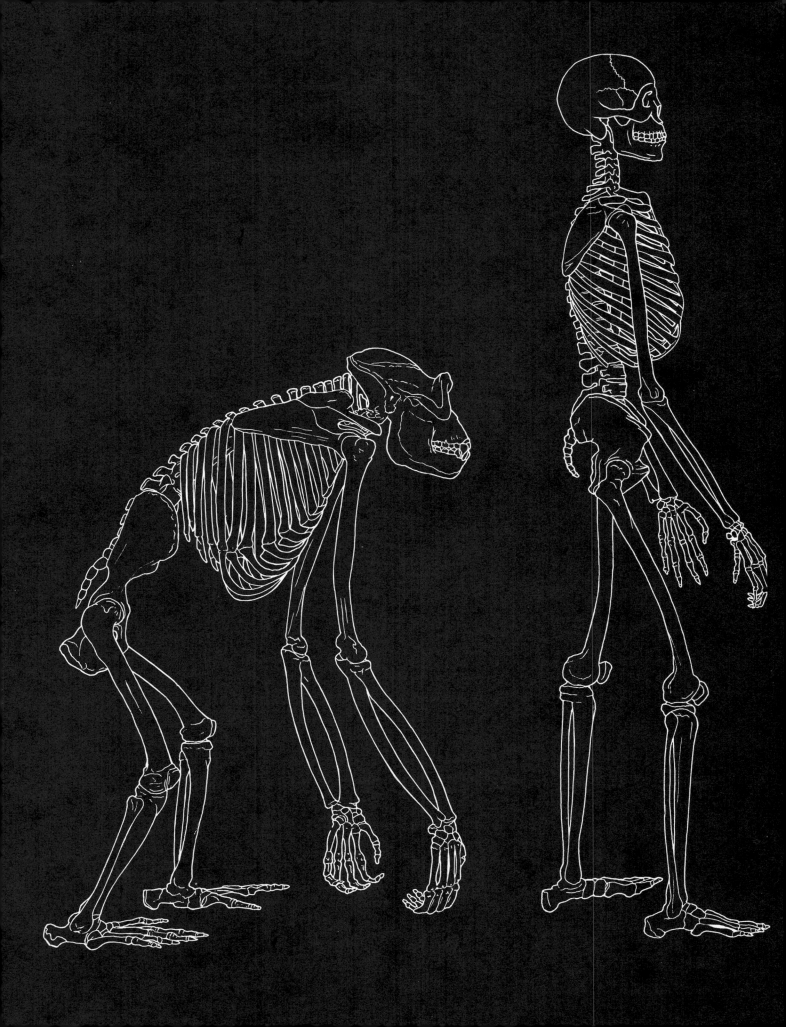